Inked

A POEM COLLECTION

SHAKTHI J

BookLeaf Publishing

India | USA | UK

Dedication

Dedicated to my loved ones, who stand with me; all the
time, against all odds.

Preface

Poems have a way of their own to talk to us. To some, it may be meaningless. To others, it might just be what they need. Writing has become my safe space and this book stands to assure that. I sincerely hope you find something that clicks for you in here, something that helps you move on in life. Because, in the end, all that matters is that we get back up, no matter how difficult the ride.

Acknowledgements

I would like to extend my deepest gratitude to everyone who has supported me on this journey. To the love that has shaped me and, the loss that has made me stronger. This book would not have been possible without you.

1. Unwhole

I can't seem to talk to you,
No matter how much I try.
Thoughts about the shared moments,
Are now just loud cries.

I hope you come and take me in,
But, would it still be a waste of time?
We talk for a while,
We love each other, then
We don't talk for months,
Broken contact for
A whole lotta while.

What do I say?
When there's this awkward silence..
Silence making us strangers,
From whatever we used to have.
What do I tell?
When there's nothing new.
Even if there was,

You don't seem to care.

To think of you as a distant memory,
Is the hardest thing to do.
Talking to you was my medicine,
To clear cache of my soul.
Because loving you,
Was all I knew.
Before we went
Unwhole.

2. Who?

I met you in my home,
I felt your gaze on me.
I loved your shiny hair,
Glistening eyes and that face,
That brought a smile upon me.

I often think about us.
How we came together,
How it all worked.
It was cinematic,
To be honest.
But, the end was bittersweet.
We parted ways
Saying very few words.
Which is why,
I write this for thee.

If we weren't meant to be,
Why were we put together?
If we weren't meant to be,

Why did we fall for each other?
If we weren't meant to be,
What was the meaning
Of all those dreams
We dreamt together?
If we weren't meant to be,
Who are you to me?
Stranger? Lover?
Probably, a keepsake
I'll cherish forever.

3. Regen

You fall so effortlessly,
After holding on for so long.
You sing so beautifully,
I forget my woes,
As soon as I hear your sound.
No one dances better than you
On the ground.
You smell so heavenly,
I could forever live with your font.
You make me happy.
Happier, on days I'm content with.
You make me feel loved,
Force of nature, as it is.
You behold such power,
You come with such strength.
One dance with you,
Is plenty enough.
To quench my dear heart's
Wish to live.

4. May you bury me

Without you,

The Sun doesn't shine,
The Water doesn't flow,
The World stands still,
All Doors closed.

You are the clay
Of sculptures I create.
You are the ink
Of letters I write .
You are the person
I want in my life,
To call my own
Even when eternity dies.

5. Strange(r)

Nightmares I see,
Lurking around my eyes.
Dark and tired,
Wanted to sleep for some time.

You looked at me with such distaste..
Should I presume
We've become strangers again?

Your words stiched the wounds
You gave me that day;
But how many stitches would I need
If I were to stay with you everyday?

You gave me flowers,
Now you crush them all day.
Used to paint me sunsets,
Now I've become the red stains.

Loved to call you summer,

Now you're lesser than plain.
My heart aches,
Seeing you become the gloom
To the rain.

6. Suitcase

The times we held our hands,
The way we connected our souls.
The roads we walked through,
The coats we wore.
The love you gave me,
The love I accepted.
The way you played with me,
The way you were bold.

The song you sang,
The way I would laugh.
The way people were jealous
Of what you and I had.
The times you wouldn't scold,
Nor would you hurt me.
The times I lay close,
And the way you would caress me.

Looks like the clock ticked away,
To a time of another dimension.

Because you seem to have changed,
From hero to villain.
The love rose I give,
Comes back as charred remains.
It has become such,
That I have become jealous of the times we lived:
So beautiful and loving.
Because, now, you've packed your suitcase
For you seem to love someone else again.

7. Hater

The way I see your face everyday,
Healing from the wounds I gave you.
Wishing I never had to give them,
But I had to.
What could've gone wrong?
There was only one way to know.
However, that's gone now.

People ask good questions when
I don't have answers at all.
You are one of the questions
I asked myself,
But my heart failed me in this round.
When I wanted it to say yes,
It said no,
When I wanted you to stay,
I told you to go.

At times I feel it's better though:
You staying away from me.

It'll give you some happiness,
It might also give you peace.
The way I make you go around in circles,
Just to push you away.
The way I keep wanting to talk,
Coz you were one of those who cared.

I hate that I brought you to your hilt,
But I'm relieved it happened the way it did.
Can't imagine what it would've been later,
When you would come to realise
I'm not the princess,
But the hater.

8. A thin line

I come from a place that fed me poison,
You were the roar,
That stopped all thoughts.
Now you've become the siren sign,
That tells me
Not to believe anyone at all.

It's been really difficult,
With you on my mind.
I don't know if I lost trust,
Or if I just need time.

Tell me how you're different,
Because I feel betrayed.
Sting rays still belong to the sharks,
I was a fool to touch one
and get preyed.

9. Drifted away

You loved me deeply.
But, I loved you in a way
So different.

"Take your time, I'll wait" you said.
But, you left before the wait
And the words in my tongue were
Left unspoken.

Expected this would happen
But, never so soon.
I loved you like a friend;
One I thought I would never lose.

10. Ambivalence

Can't you see I hate it when,
You do every single thing I want? .
Told me I'm stronger than
What I think of myself,
Like you've known me for long.

To believe you is the hardest task,
Because of the paths,
I've been through before.

You throw me in the fire,
Soon take me out.
Hold me in the city lights and
Hug me tight,
Until I can't breathe anymore.

People tell me I'm falling in the wrong place,
But falling never felt so right.
I'm scared to be blinded,
But with you, it seems just fine.

To know you is one thing,
To have you is another.
To love you is one thing,
To be loved by you, another.

11. Muddled

I love you in the dark.
In the mornings, I'm afraid.
What if you showed different colours in the sunlight,
Like several others did on several days?

You talk like milk dripping from
A cut to the rubber tree.
Calculated words,
Slow and steady.

I stood there listening,
Now unconscious, I lay.
Stuck with emotions in the end,
None of which I can explain.

12. Complication

You and I were friends,
Until you came up and
Asked me "the" question.

To know you was hard,
But, to love you was way harder.
I knew it then but
I said yes, coz it didn't matter.

If only you were
As easy as your voice,
As effortless as your words,
As calm as I thought your mind was.

To actually know what goes on inside your head
Was nearly impossible.
I used to wonder:
If you ever really thought of me,
If you ever really missed me.

Because one day,
I heard you had another flower.
And I found myself standing there,
Baffled.
Coz you claimed us to be friends,
When we were clearly
More than that.

13. Bittersweet

It's bittersweet,
Seeing our parents
Grow old.

It's bittersweet,
How well we do
And suddenly we don't.

It's bittersweet,
Dark chocolate, I mean.

It's bittersweet,
Knowing we came from dust
And to dust we shall return.

It's bittersweet,
Thinking about how
We knew each other.

Which now seems to be,
A long time ago.

14. An apology

She asked him,
"Do you not love me?"
And he replied,
"If I did not love you,
I wouldn't have come this far."

"What happened then?
Why do you want to leave?"

He said,
"You are the sun,
And I, the moon.
It's in my destiny
To love you from afar."

15. Lies

Say it.

Tell me you don't love me,
Just don't lie to my face.

Tell me you'd never love me,
Because you don't know how.

Tell me I'll find a better person,
Because you know you're not.

Tell me you don't love me,
And tell it to me now.
Because you knew
It would hurt me,
If it went on too long.

16. No Calls

It's been seven days,
Since we last talked.
And I just know,
I'll have to let you go now.

17. Away

I was certain of you.
You were certain of that.
But, you broke it off,
Like you never cared.

I called you first,
I called you last.
Longed for a call from you,
Before you sailed apart.

18. Legends of Belief

My musings.

Proper love.
The kind we see in rom-coms.
I would be lying
If I said I didn't dream of it at all.

Fairy tales.
The Disney ones.
I would talk to the
Curtains, tiles, bottles and fridge,
"Oh prince charming!
Where are you now?"

In the stories
My grandma tells me,
Of Gods and Goddesses,
Kings and Queens.
I loved to play the part,
And imagine it all.

She would tell me it's real,
I would follow along.
Talked for hours,
Played for more.
Filled the world with colours,
Only we could see somehow.

19. White paint

Painted a canvas
With you in it.
I see you and cry,
Because we were more than this.

Looking into your eyes,
All I see are empty promises;
Of what we were,
Of what we could've been.

Was feeling bad about
What I lost,
Then realised,
It was
You, who lost me.

So I painted it white again.

20. Dear heart, calm down will you?

"People don't seem to understand,
What it means to be
The one she's looking at."

And in line
With the time he said that,
My heart went,
"OH. MY. GOD."

21. The Art and the Muse

Art is what I create,
A Muse is who you are.
I kept you on a pedestal,
Made you an ideal bod.

You asked me to paint you,
And I painted you as
Something you're not.
Took me quite a while,
To finally cognise, that
You were just the apple
That got to the table that day,
On some fateful night.

That painting, though?
That, was all mine.

22. Her.

Sunset on a deserted beach,
Moonlit forest, midnight bower.
A chill breeze on a winter evening,
Snowflakes falling every hour.

You've been here with me through it all.
Childhood summers, family gatherings,
Love, fights, hobbies and what not?

All those memories,
Now, stand rediscovered.
It's been you and me,
Always and forever.

And just like that, we heal.